Mother Earth's Quilt Sampler

Appliqué Patterns Inspired by Mother Earth and Her Children

Sieglinde Schoen Smith

Breckling Press

Library of Congress Cataloging-in-Publication Data

Schoen Smith, Sieglinde,

Mother Earth's quilt sampler : appliqué patterns inspired by Mother

Earth and her children / Sieglinde Schoen Smith.

p. cm.

ISBN 978-1-933308-22-7

1. Quilting--Patterns. 2. Appliqué--Patterns. 3.

Embroidery--Patterns. I. Olfers, Sibylle, 1881-1916 Etwas von den

Wurzelkindern. English. II. Title.

TT835.S34847 2008

746.46'041--dc22

2008034114

This book was set in Garamond Premier Pro, Erasmus, Carlton, and Windlass
Patterns inspired by Etwas von den Wurzelkindern by Sibylle von Olfers, 1906
Editorial and art direction by Anne Knudsen
Interior and cover design by Maria Mann
Photography by Cathy Meals

Published by Breckling Press
283 N. Michigan St, Elmhurst, IL 60126

Printed and bound in China
International Standard Book Number (ISBN 13): 978-1-933308-22-7

I was born in the very southern part of Germany during World War II, the second youngest of five sisters. As a tot, I had no toys of my own to play with. There were hand-me-downs from my sisters, but they were of no interest to me. I remember how badly I wanted something to love that was *mine* alone! And I found it. In fact, I found a whole world outdoors that I could make my very own. The flowers, with their tiny Spring buds opening to the first rays of sun, the trees arching high above me, and the clouds rushing by on an Autumn breeze were all part of my playground. My world had creatures in it, too. The ladybugs and beetles were my friends, and I let them crawl through my fingers or nestle in the palm of my hand. We had such conversations, the bugs and I! With my sisters away at school, I made my own games in the garden, not knowing I was also making memories that would last a lifetime.

As all little children must, I grew up, but my early love of nature stayed with me. As a young woman, I moved to the United States in 1963 and had a family of my own. Many years later, I took up quilting. Now, I had learned needlework and embroidery as a child from my grandmother, but quilting was new to me and I looked around for ideas. This is when those sweet memories of childhood rushed back to me. My inspiration was the wondrous world of nature as I first saw it all those years ago.

To my surprise, one of my first quilts, *Mother Earth and Her Children*, inspired by a German storybook I had loved as a child, was honored with first place in a major international quilt show. A children's picture book by the same name quickly followed. Something in the faces of those sweet children I had recreated in fabric and embroidery resonated with quilters, who soon asked me for patterns so that they could make Mother Earth quilts of their own. This book is my answer. The four small quilt featured here are windows into the seasons of Mother Earth. I hope that you will enjoy looking through them.

Sieglinde Schoen Smith

Cont

Techniques

"With needles, scissors, spools of thread,
They measure and cut, full steam ahead."

I am a self-taught quilter and have only recently taken up this wonderful craft. Of course, I learned to sew and embroider when I was very young. My grandmother sat me down at the age of 3 and helped me make my very first embroidery project. Times were hard when I was growing up in post-war Germany, and my sisters and I spent much of our time sewing everything that was needed for our household as well as making little gifts for each other. Every year I gave my Papa hand-knitted socks for Christmas and Mama acquired quite a collection of hand-embroidered aprons.

Still, it was not until much later in my life, after the loss of my son Steven, that I turned to quilting for comfort and to keep my hands and mind busy. I started with a simple pillow, embroidered with forget-me-nots. Soon, I adapted the same pillow design to a quilt, which, at my husband's urging, I entered into a quilt show. To my surprise, it won the handcraft ward.

Needing a new project, I turned to a children's book that was my favorite as a child, *Etwas von den Wurzelkindern*, which translates rather awkwardly into English as *Something About the Root Children*. A classic of German children's literature, it was written in 1906 by a young princess, Sibylle von Olfers, who would soon afterwards enter a holy convent. The book charmingly portrays Mother Earth's little children, asleep under the tree roots during Winter, only to awaken in the Spring and become the flowers of Summer. I still loved the rich but delicately drawn illustrations, full of flowers, butterflies, beetles, and all of God's littlest creatures. I wondered if I could transfer the entire story onto a quilt.

Now, I knew little of either traditional or modern quilting methods. I didn't have a big collection of quilter's tools. I looked at the pictures in the book, searched out some fabrics I thought would suit the task, then sat down to work. In the pages that follow, I will do my best to describe my techniques, which are very slight variations on good old-fashioned hand-sewing methods. People tell me that modern tools and techniques make for faster, more accurate work, but I'm not convinced. I completed my quilt, which I named *Mother Earth and Her Children*, in a year and a day. When it first went on display, it won Best-in-Show at America's most prestigious quilt exhibition, International Quilt Festival. It went on to win four more national prizes the same year. So you tell me, can traditional needlework techniques like mine help you complete a quilt quickly, accurately, and beautifully? I hope you will give it a try!

Supply Kit

- Tracing paper: Buy 11" x 17" sheets or larger, if you can find them
- Graphite transfer paper: Buy a roll of 18" x 36" or large sheets (buy black for use with light fabrics; white for dark fabrics)
- Fine tip permanent markers
- Fine tip ballpoint pens
- Water-soluble fabric marker
- Appliqué needles: Choose the smallest size you can thread. I use Roxanne's size 12 betweens
- Thread to your liking: I use YLI's 100 percent silk thread, matched to the color of the appliqués
- Scissors (for cutting fabric)
- Small fine point scissors (for clipping seams and cutting threads)
- Glass head straight pins
- Ruler
- Thimble
- Batting: I like thin cotton batting
- Black cotton piping: I use ½" single-fold bias piping
- Embroidery hoop: I use a 4" wooden hoop.
- Embroidery needles: Choose a small size, either size 10 or 11; I use John James Big Eye quilting needles, size 11 (JJ 12511)
- Single-strand embroidery floss in colors of your choosing: I prefer DMC 6-ply

Fabrics

For the projects in *Mother Earth's Quilt Sampler* I used commercially purchased batiks almost exclusively. I love the variations in color across a single piece of fabric. To my mind, batiks are perfect for recreating scenes from nature; the subtle changes in hues, shadows, and highlights mirror the thousands of shades Mother Nature gives us. I also love that batiks are so lightweight. This makes them easy to sew and quilt, even through the seam allowances necessary for appliqué. Their weave is very dense, making it possible to use tiny seam allowances.

The only non-batik fabric I use is the bright white for Mother Earth's hat and apron, plus a few other small details. I found that even the brightest white cottons looked too dry next to more colorful batiks. I searched for something with a little extra sparkle. Finally I settled on 100 percent white polyester, which gives the shine I wanted. Of course, choose any fabric that pleases you—the quilt is yours, after all.

When shopping for batiks, buy small quantities of as many hues as you can find. For my projects, it is better to have 50 small scraps that are all different, than a few half yards of a handful of fabrics. Instead of choosing one yellow, choose five shades of yellow. Find as many blues, greens, tans, and browns as you can—these are Mother Nature's palette and you will always find uses for them.

Transferring the Design to Fabric

After buying this book and template set, you must promise me that you will *never* cut your master templates apart. These will be your guide as you plan and carry out each project. Always keep them safe for future use. This is how best to use the master templates.

Trace

1 Choose the patterns for the quilt you plan to make. Place a cloth over them and iron lightly to remove the folds. Lay the pattern pieces for the picture window and the borders flat on a large, sturdy surface.

2 Using invisible tape, tape together sheets of tracing paper so that you are able to cover the entire template with an inch to spare around all outer edges. Place the tracing paper over the picture window design. If needed, tape the tracing paper to the table so that it does not shift during tracing. Smooth out any air pockets or wrinkles before taping. With a firm hand and a fine-tip permanent marker, start tracing the design. Copy the background design onto the tracing paper first. For the Fall quilt, for instance, working from top to bottom, start with the lines where the sky meets the cave top and the distant meadows. Moving down, draw the green grass, followed by the curves of the river, and so on to the bottom of the quilt until you have traced the entire background of the image. Next, trace all the details, big and small, from the children's dresses to the tiniest bugs and beetles.

Step 2

Sieglinde's Secret

I prefer to complete the entire tracing, including all the tiny details, before moving on. If you are less patient and can't wait to pick up your needle to sew, complete the background, then choose a small area of the design to transfer to fabric. Once you have satisfied your desire to see part of the design in fabric, go back to your tracing table.

Transfer to Fabric

3 When the design (or the portion of the design you are working on) is completely traced, remove the tracing and set the master template aside. Choose fabrics for the background of the image. (In Fall, for instance, you will need blue for the sky, green-brown for the cave top, light brown for the distant meadows, green for the grass, blue for the river, and so on moving down the quilt. Beginning at the top of the design, place the sky fabric right side up on the table and cover it completely with graphite paper, ink side down. Place the tracing on top, right side up. With a firm hand and a fine-tip ballpoint pen, draw over the lines on the tracing, transferring them to the fabric beneath. Draw over every line, including the smallest details. When you have finished the sky, move on to the next background piece, continuing until the entire design is transferred onto the background pieces. Make sure that the line that divides the sky from the cave top, for instance, is on the blue sky fabric as well as the brown/green cave top fabric. These should be a perfect match.

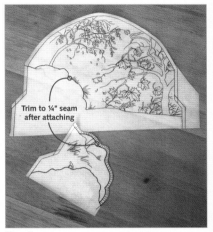

Trim to ¼" seam after attaching

Step 3

Sew the Background

4 Lay out the pieces that make up the background on a flat surface. Check to make sure that the common lines they share are a perfect match. For instance, in Fall, check that the line at the bottom edge of the sky exactly matches the line at the top edge of the cave top and the top edge of the distant meadows. Check that the bottom edge of the cave top exactly matches the top line of the cave interior, the bottom edge of the distant meadows exactly matches the top edge of the grass, and so on down the quilt. (More detail is provided with each quilt.) Rough-cut each background piece first, leaving an inch or so of fabric beyond each marked line. Once the line is drawn and you are sure of it, trim the top fabric (the piece you will appliqué) to ¼". Where the sewing line curves, clip into the top fabric, just two or three threads short of the stitching line, every ⅛" around the curve. As you sew around the curve, turn under just ⅛" flap at a time. This will help the sewn line lie flat. Appliqué as directed in the pattern instructions along the entire lengths of these lines, until the entire background piece is complete. Trim the bottom fabric (the piece you appliquéd onto) from 1" to ¼".

Trim 1" seam to ¼ after attaching the next piece

Step 4

Mark though graphite paper onto fabric

Transfer onto background fabric as well as appliqué fabric

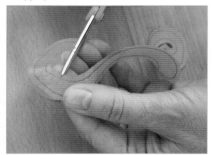

Clip close into the curves.

Position the appliqué motif on top of the background.

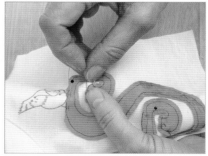

Begin appliqué

Transfer and Sew the Appliqués

5 Check the pattern instructions and decide which portion of the design to begin with. I recommend starting with the bottom 6" or so of the design, working across its entire width. Choose fabrics for each element of the design. (Each pattern includes a list of suggested fabric colors.) As with the background pieces, place the fabric for the first motif right side up on the table, cover it with graphite paper, and put the tracing on top. With a fine-tip ballpoint pen, draw over the lines of the motif you wish to transfer.

6 Add a ⅛" or smaller seam allowance around all fabric motifs before cutting. At the curves, clip into the fabric, just two or three threads short of the stitching line, every ⅛" around the curve. This will help the sewn line lie flat.

7 Once you have cut them all, lay out all the fabric pieces you will need on top of the marked background. Make sure they match up exactly. If in doubt, double-check against the master template, then fix your marking lines accordingly.

8 Use a single pin to attach the first appliqué motif to the background. Position the pin opposite your beginning stitching point. Use thread in a color to match your appliqué and the smallest needle you can thread. Turn under one ⅛" flap at a time. Making sure that the traced stitching line is just barely turned under, catch only a couple of threads at the edge of the motif and stitch it in place.

9 Complete the rest of the picture-window design in the same way, using colors that please you. If you like and as you become more confident, add flowers, bugs, and butterflies of your own to make your quilt unique!

10 Follow the instructions in the patterns to cut and piece the wide outer border and attach the picture-window to it. Add appliqué motifs in exactly the same way described here.

Sieglinde's Secret

Sometimes, it may be difficult to tell from the photographs which of the smaller pieces are appliquéd and which are embroidered. As a general rule, the children's faces, hair, hands, legs, and feet are embroidered; their clothes are appliqué. Since the necks are so tiny, I generally include the neck when marking and cutting the appliqués for the dresses. I then embroider right over the appliqué. Most of the larger bug and beetle pieces are appliqué; the bugs' legs, feet, antennae, and portions of the wings are usually embroidery. The larger flower, leaf, and stem pieces are appliqué; the smaller details and buds are embroidery. Of course, you can embroider as much or as little as you please—the decisions are all up to you!

Adding Embroidery

Embroidery adds a lovely, textured look that brings the children's faces to life. I use just four embroidery styles, all described here. For all embroidery, I use a single strand of DMC 6-ply embroidery floss and a size 10 or 11 needle. I recommend using a small embroidery hoop—mine is just 4" wide and is made of wood.

Layered embroidery

I use a technique called *layered embroidery* to embroider the children's faces and other large areas like butterfly wings and the bodies of my little wasps. I grew up near a convent in Germany and I learned embroidery from the Sisters. My layered embroidery technique gives the children's faces a nice, soft texture; it also allows subtle shading that gives the faces natural coloring. Use single-strand embroidery floss and a stitch length of no more than ⅜."

1   Lightly mark the area to be embroidered as shown. Use a water-soluble marker. This will help keep all your stitches going in the same direction.

2   Begin at one end of the area to be embroidered and make a very dense row of even-sized satin stitches across to the other end of the design. Get the stitches as close together as you can.

3   Make a second row adjacent to the first. Do not allow a gap to show between the two rows; to achieve this smooth effect, the ends of your stitches will jut between the stitches in the first row. Use the same color or, if the design requires a new color, change thread. (In the sample shown, I started the second row with pink, then switched back to cream when I reached the end of the cheek line.)

Step 1

Step 2

Step 3

Step 4

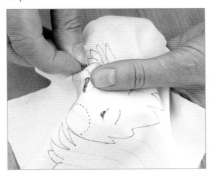

Embroidery stitch

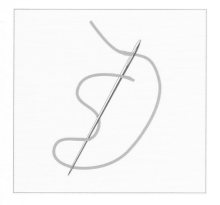

French knot

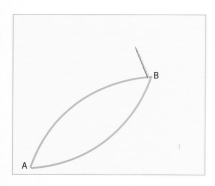

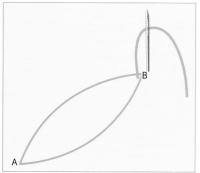

Lazy daisy stitch

4 Make a third row, this time stitching over the "seam" between the first and second rows. Your stitches will sink down into the previous layers, blending invisibly into them.

5 Continue adding rows, overlapping each "seam" with a same-color layer and alternating colors as necessary until the design area is filled.

The trick to layered embroidery is to fool the eye to the point where you can no longer distinguish the rows of embroidery but see only one continuous surface. Keeping your stitches very close together and avoiding any gaps between the rows will help.

French Knot

I use French knots for details like flower buds, the eyes of butterflies, and the balls at the ends of a dragonfly's antennae.

Knot the thread, then bring the needle up through the fabric from the back at an angle. If you prefer a denser knot, use double-strand floss rather than single strand. With your left thumb, hold the thread taut against the fabric, about ½" away from the entry point. Twist the needle around that ½" length of thread two or three times (depending on the size of knot you want). Push the needle back through the fabric, very close to but not into the entry point.

Lazy Daisy Stitch

Sometimes I use a simple lazy daisy stitch to embellish flower centers. Knot the thread, then bring the needle up through the fabric from the back. Come up at A and make a small loop, holding it against the fabric with your left thumb. Go down as close as possible to A, but not into it. Do not pull the loop through the fabric. Come up at B and make a small stitch over the loop, holding it in place. Bring the needle back up at A. Repeat, making a second lazy daisy stitch. Continue working from center point A until you have made a lazy daisy stitch flower.

Outlining with Stem Stitch

Once all the appliqué and embroidery is complete, I outline each motif in black with stem stitch embroidery. I stitch around the embroidered faces and bugs as well as around the fabric appliqués. I also use stem stitch for drawing the antennae of butterflies, spider webs, and other fine details.

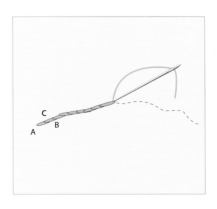

Work as close as possible to the edge of the appliqué motif, but stitch into the background, not the motif. Knot the thread, then bring the needle up from the back to the front at you starting point (A).

Make a slant stitch about ⅛" long to B, then re-insert the needle, angling it back toward A.

Come up at C, about half way along the previous stitch. Repeat, continuing around the entire motif. Exit at the back of the work and knot off.

Making the Borders

Each quilt has two borders: the narrow border around the picture-window, and the wide outer border.

Narrow Border

Soft-fold the bias piping in half lengthwise. Working from the back, sew the folded binding to the back of the picture window background, so that only ⅛" shows at the front. Continue around the entire picture window.

Notice that there a part of each picture window that overlaps onto the wide outer border. On Summer, for instance, the white dragonfly wing on the right overlaps, as do the blue flower and green leaf at the left. Begin the border at one of these overlapping areas so that you are able to hide your starting and stopping points and do not need to miter the border.

Wide Outer Border

Piece together a rectangle of border fabric to measure 30" x 38". Pin the completed picture window to the center, using the quilt photograph as a guide. Space the pins ½" apart or closer to ensure a flat, even border.

Inside and butting up to the narrow border of the picture window, make a single row of stem-stitch in gold embroidery thread. Work around the entire perimeter of the picture-window, making sure to sew through all layers and attaching the picture window to the wide border.

Complete any unfinished appliqué that extends over the picture-window border. Turn the work over and trim away the excess green fabric behind the picture window to reduce bulk.

Lazy daisy stitch and French knots

Quilting pattern

Finishing the Quilt

You may choose any style you please for binding your quilt. Because batik fabrics are hard to needle, I always use the thinnest batting I can find. My preference is Mountain Mist's 100 percent cotton batting, which needles very easily. I quilt with Mettler cotton thread to match the fabric. Use a needle that is comfortable for you. I like to use the smallest, finest needles that fit the thread used. The smaller the needle the easier the needle glides through the fabric. I also use Thread Heaven thread conditioner and protectant.

If you look on the back of one of my embroidered appliqué quilts, you will see that I leave many areas unquilted. Rather than struggle with appliqué seams, I quilt only the open areas of the background, between motifs. Since the quilts in this book are small, I work without a hoop or frame, quilting on my lap. Do whatever is comfortable for you!

1 Measure your quilt across the center, horizontally and vertically. Piece a rectangle of backing fabric that matches these measurements, plus an extra inch on all sides. For the quilts in this book, the rectangle will be about 31" x 39". Add a layer of batting with the same measurements.

2 Lay out the backing on a table top, and position the batting then the quilt top over it, smoothing each layer out as you go. Pin the layers together, using one pin at least every square inch. Baste the entire quilt, holding the layers together, and remove the pins.

3 The quilting pattern for open areas inside the picture window is a ⅜" grid crossed twice diagonally. I usually quilt without marking, but if you need to, lightly mark the pattern onto the open areas of the quilt top using a water-soluble marker. Do not quilt over the appliqués or the embroidery. The wide border is quilted with a simple ⅜" square grid.

Sieglinde's Secret

Remember, I told you I do not have a big collection of quilting tools? Well, when it came time to make the scalloped border, I looked around to see what I could find. In the kitchen I spotted a little saucer that looked just the right size. If you wish to do the same, measure your quilt carefully so you are certain to make the first scallops at the very center of the top, bottom, and sides of the quilt.

Binding

The soft-edge scalloped binding lends a sense of texture to the quilt. Use the border patterns in the template set to create your border. Before you begin, measure your quilt carefully to make sure the patterns are an exact fit. If they do not quite match, either trim your quilt to the correct size or adjust the template pattern to fit your quilt.

1   Start by transferring the scalloped border pattern onto your quilt using graphite paper (see pages 2 to 3). Trim the quilt to a ¼" seam allowance beyond your marked line.

2   Cut a 2" bias strip of fabric. Sew bias pieces together to form one long strip, long enough to go all around the outside edge of the quilt. Fold the strip in half lengthwise and press, matching the raw edges exactly. Leave about a 3" to 4" unfolded at one end.

3   By hand or machine, start to attach the folded end of the strip to the top edge of the front of the quilt at the highest part of the scallop. Sew around the front of the quilt, making sure to sew into each inside curve of each scallop. Clip each inside curve exactly to the sewing line, being careful not to cut the sewn curve.

4   Once you get to about 4" to 6" from the end, open the bias strip. Measure how much of the strip is still needed. Trim to the correct length, plus ¼". Turn that ¼" under, fold in half again and fingerpress. Sew the end in place, slightly overlapping the starting point.

5   Fold the unsewn long edge of the bias toward the back of the quilt and attach with small appliqué stitches.

When the quilting is finished, I add a pretty but unnecessary finishing touch. I add diagonal lines of stem-stitch across the entire back of the quilt. I make sure my needle goes through the backing only, not through to the front. The diagonal lines are spaced about an inch apart.

   If you need more help with finishing, basting, quilting, and binding refer to one of the many quilting books devoted to this topic. If you plan to display your quilt, attach a sleeve so that you can hang it. And don't forget to attach a label with your name and date, so that everyone can know how clever you are!

"And when fair Spring arrives on time,
A merry group soon comes alive.
Ladybugs, lilies, tall blades of grass,
Emerge on the earth in a joyous mass."

"Mama, see! The pussy willow is already waking up!" I ran to show my mother how the hard shells on the willow branch were bursting open to display the soft white furry blooms inside. This could only mean one thing–the Spring sun was warming the earth again, stirring all of nature's surprises.

Finished size: 29¾" x 37½", including binding

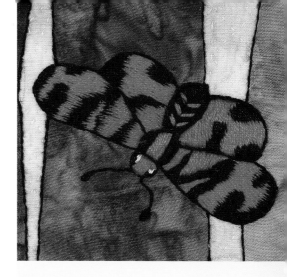

Materials

All quantities are generous so that you can cut large shapes from a single piece of fabric, wherever possible. You will have plenty of leftover fabric to play with! I use variegated batiks for everything except the white dresses and snowbells. There, believe it or not, I use white polyester. I like its sheen and it makes those white dresses really pop.

Background

Sky: ½ yard light blue
Grass: ½ yard light green

Appliqués

Trees: ¼ yard each of at least six shades from cream to dark

Dresses, pants, cloak, and shoes: ¼ yard each of white and blue; ⅛ yard or large scrap of light green

Foliage: ⅛ yard or large scraps in at least five shades of green

Toadstools: Scraps of bright red and cream

Flowers, bugs and butterflies: Scraps in as many colors as you can find!

Letters: Scraps of light blue, pink, lilac, green, and orange.

Plus

Narrow picture-window border: 2½ yards dark brown or black single-fold bias piping

Wide border: 1 yard dark green

Backing: 1yard, any color

Binding: 5 yards bright yellow single-fold bias binding

Embroidery: Single-ply embroidery thread in black and white, as well as shades of silver grey, gold, yellow, orange, brown, cream, pink, lilac, teal, and whatever additional colors you please

Note: See page 2 for help in choosing fabrics.

When I was little, we lived in the last house at the edge of our small rural town. It was just ten minutes walk from the river Danube. Yet the walk in the opposite direction was of more interest to me. A narrow dirt road wound its way along a fast running brook, twisting from the meadows and fields to the mountains, the beautiful Fore-Alb. Day after day I would roam through the tall trees, my eyes open for discoveries.

As soon as the snow melted, off I would go. I'd hunt for moss to build an Easter-nest in the yard. Of course, I would have to have the softest, prettiest nest in order for bunny to leave goodies for me on Easter morning. The year before, when there were no eggs in my nest (eggs were a rare commodity in post-war Germany), Papa had told me why: A little Easter bunny boy had tripped on my nest and spilled his paints! Then Papa drew a picture for me – a boy bunny delivering brightly colored eggs into my nest.

I closed my eyes tight and hoped that the Easter bunny would make that picture come true this year! Hope and prayer were my best allies, since times were hard.

One of my favorite spots was an opening in the woods where the

ground was carpeted with delicate blue violets. The aroma was so sweet! I would pick a bouquet to surprise Mama. She had always told me that flowers are the smiles of God, so I knew she would not mind if I picked them. From my hiding place, I could watch the oxen or horses draw plows across the fields, as farmers got an early start on the year's harvest.

Tiny flowers I knew as "goose daisies" were an early sign of Spring. These bright white and yellow wildflowers grow close to the ground and I loved to run my tiny fingers through them. I would sit among them and choose the prettiest of all to make my daisy chains, splitting a stem with a fingernail and carefully sliding the next stem through it. Oh, the garlands, bracelets, and tiaras I would make! No princess could be happier!

Early each Spring, a wild stork would fly back to his nest on top of our City Hall. I would spy him flying low over the woods, his new bride following close behind, and I would wonder where he had been. Once he had reclaimed his home, I knew it was time for the swallows and the butterflies to arrive, too. And how about my beloved little teddy-bears-of-the-air, the bumblebees!

Mama gave me a little part of her garden for my own. It was surrounded

Make the Picture Window

1   Follow the directions on pages 2 to 3 to transfer the entire image inside the picture window onto fabric. Trace the pattern onto tracing paper first, then use graphite paper to transfer the design to fabric. Work carefully, tracing one section at a time.

Background

2   Begin with the line between the sky and the grass. Since the edge of the grass fabric is hidden by appliquéd tree trunks, follow the line of the tree trucks to see where the grass ends. Transfer this line onto both blue and green fabric. Check against the master template to make sure that both fabric lines match *exactly*. Trim each piece to a ⅛" seam allowance. (See page 4 for help with cutting and seam allowances.) Turn under the seam as you go, and appliqué the upper edge of the green grass piece on top of the blue sky piece. You will need to clip curves as you sew, so that the appliqué lies neatly on top of the blue fabric. (See page 4 for help with appliqué.)

Sieglinde's Secret

I prefer to completely finish tracing and transferring the image to fabric before I begin any sewing. If you are less patient and can't wait to pick up your needle, complete the entire background, then choose distinct areas of the quilt to concentrate on first. Take care to note, however, which pieces should be appliquéd before others (see page 4).

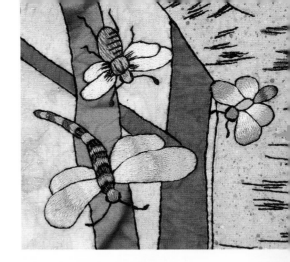

3   Check the size of the background against the master template. It should measure about 20¾" wide x 27" from the bottom to the center top. Allow an extra ½" seam allowance all around, then trim away any excess fabric. If necessary, turn the work over and trim away any excess fabric to a scant ⅛" seam allowance. This will help reduce any bulky layers your needle has to work through later when you quilt.

Appliqués

4   As you become more familiar with my techniques, you will be able to choose any part of the design to begin your appliqué. Until you have completed one quilt, I suggest you begin by building the picture from the bottom up. Start by studying the bottom 7" or so of the picture window, across the entire width (to the top of the head of the blue girl at the right). If you have not completed tracing and transferring the motifs in this area to fabric, do so now. Working from left to right, cut pieces (adding a ⅛" seam allowance or smaller for the tiny pieces) for the blue flower, the leaves, the three white dresses, both blue dresses, the log, snail, and butterfly, the green shoes, pants, and cloak, the blue flower and leaves, the toadstools, and the dull green patch in the bottom right corner. Cut the entire length of each long tree trunk. (Note that the children's faces, hair, hands, and feet, plus the gold-brown ferns are embroidered; you will not have to cut appliqués for these pieces.) Study the photograph to figure out the appliqué sequence (see also page 4). Here, for instance, the leftmost blue dress is appliquéd before the white girls and the leaves; the log before the snail, the snail's body before the shell; the lowest tree trunks before the rightmost blue girl and the green boy; and the toadstool stems before the caps. Appliqué only the bottom parts of the white dresses and the green cloaks, leaving the rest unfinished for now (since they will overlap pieces you have not yet sewn down).Turn the work over and trim away any excess fabric to reduce bulk.

5   Move to the next 6" section across the width of the pattern (just above the topmost snowbell at the left). Working from left to right, cut pieces (adding ⅛" seam allowance) for the leaves and snowbells, plus any other tree trunks you have not yet cut. Continue appliquéing any tree trunks left unfinished from the previous step. Appliqué any new tree trunks, then add the leaves, then the snowbells at the left. Finish the green boy at the right. Turn the work over and trim away any excess fabric to reduce bulk.

6   Complete the remaining top section of the picture window in the same way. Appliqué the darker tree trunks first, followed by the lighter ones. This will give visual depth to your forest of trees, since the first sewn pieces recede from the eye and the last-sewn pieces advance (see page 4). (Note that the butterflies are all embroidered, not appliqué.) Turn the work over and trim away any excess fabric to reduce bulk.

by tall green rhubarb plants. Their humungous leaves served as a playhouse for the bugs, snails, and other critters who came to visit. In Spring, my garden was a magical kingdom of primroses and crocuses. Mama would give me a batch of tiny cress seeds and I would position them carefully to spell out my name. As the days passed, I would watch my name grow in delicate green strands, and all the world would know that this was Sieglinde's garden!

Snails were special guests in my little garden. I would search out the snails with the prettiest houses packed on their backs. Taking out my toothbrush, I would brush the shells until they gleamed in the sunlight. I never used soap and water, since that would foam up a storm! When the snails were ready, I would tuck the poor things into bed under the leaves of the rhubarb plants, where the other bug visitors were already asleep in their matchbox beds. When I was just a little older, I wondered if God would be angry with me for playing so hard with His tiny creatures.

On my daily excursions into the woods, I would always wonder about the way things worked in nature. Where does the color inside flowers come from? Why did God make so many colors? How do

Embroider the Picture Window

7   Complete the layered embroidery of the children's faces, hair, hands, legs and feet. Complete all other layered embroidery, including the butterflies, stems, the brown flowerets at the far right, plus the detailing on the toadstool. (For help with layered embroidery, see page 5.)

8   With single-strand black embroidery thread and stem stitch, outline all elements of the design. Outline around each child, each tree trunk, each bug, each flower, each reed, and each stem. Study the photographs to see exactly where to outline. (For help with stem stitch embroidery, see page 7).

9   Use stem stitch to create the ferns at the center and far left and right, plus the sprigs of grass in the foreground. Add details to the butterfly wings, the snail, and the flowers and leaves. Add French knots to the ends of the butterfly antannae (see page 6).

snails move if they have no legs? How do they shrink their entire bodies inside their shells so quickly when touched? How do ants milk aphids? How does a stork find his nest again after flying so many miles? And if papa stork dies on the journey, does his young son, who has never made the flight before, know how to find the same nest? I know, I know, there are scientific answers for all these questions. But in my mind, it is all God's magic.

Not every day was a play-day. On rainy days my dear grandmother–Oma, as I called her–took me under her wing. I would sit on a stool at her feet and she would teach me how to embroider. She would sketch out a design for me and watch me make the stitches. Over and over, she would say, "You did very well, but, you know, it is not pretty yet." With that, her scissors would quickly take my work out, and I started over. Again and again, I sewed the same design until it was pretty in Oma's eyes. Only many years later did I realize what the dear lady had taught me. I mastered embroidery, of course, but I also learned patience and the joy of accomplishment when something turns out pretty, because, you know, today I can see through Oma's eyes.

Make the Borders

13 See page 7 for directions on how to complete the narrow picture window border.

14 See page 7 for directions on how to make the wide outer border and attach it to the picture window.

15 Follow the directions on pages 2 to 3 to transfer the letters and flowers inside the wide border onto fabric. Trace onto tracing paper first, then use graphite paper to transfer the marks to fabric. Work carefully, tracing one section at a time.

16 Cut pieces (adding ⅛" seam allowance) for the letters at the top of the quilt, then appliqué them carefully in place. Do the same for the butterflies, caterpillar, flowers and leaves. Note any overlaps, particularly where the leaf at the left overlaps at the angle of the picture-window border.

17 In the same way, cut pieces then appliqué the snail, flowers, leaves, and buds along the left border and the bottom left corner.

18 Use layered embroidery to complete any detailing like the flower center, details on the butterflies, and the yellow flowers in the bottom right of the border. Use stem stitch, lazy daisy stitch, and French knots to complete other details. (See pages 6 to 7). Use stem stitch for the sprigs of grass and other fine details. Stem stitch your autograph at the bottom right.

19 Follow the directions on pages 8 to 9 to add backing, quilt the entire piece, scallop the outer border, and add binding.

Summer

"Beside the brook, these earthly tots
Skip among forget-me-nots.
Like little kings all day they play,
On lily pads they sail away."

I have special June memories of going into
the forest with my favorite sister Hannelore
to pick wild strawberries. Every year
we found little ways to celebrate Papa's
name day – or Saints day – even when he
was away from us, and a strawberry hunt
usually started off the festivities. Oh what
fun we had! Armed with metal milk

Finished size: 29¾" x 37½", including binding

Summer

Sieglinde 07

Materials

All quantities are generous so that you can cut large shapes from a single piece of fabric, wherever possible. You will have plenty of leftover fabric to play with! I use variegated batiks for everything except the white dragonfly wings and the white petals on the violets. There, I used shiny white polyester, which works well because of its sheen and texture.

Background

Sky: ½ yard light blue

Grass: ½ yard light green

Appliqués

Mountains: ½ yard gray

Pond: ¼ yard light blue

Pondside: ½ yard dull green

Reeds: ⅛ yard each of at least four shades of brown and green

Dresses and boy clothes: ⅛ yard each or large scraps of yellow, bright green, dull green, light blue, purple, orange, and pink

Foliage: ⅛ yard or large scraps in at least three shades of green

Flowers, bugs and butterflies: Scraps in as many colors as you can find!

Letters: Scraps of bright orange, blue, yellow, red, green, and purple

Plus

Narrow picture-window border: 2½ yards dark brown single-fold bias piping

Wide border: 1 yard light green

Backing: 1 yard, any color

Binding: 5 yards blue single-fold bias binding

Embroidery: Single-ply embroidery thread in black and white, as well as shades of silver grey, gold, yellow, orange, brown, cream, pink, lilac, teal, and whatever additional colors you please

Note See page 2 for help in choosing fabrics.

cans, mine smaller than my sister's, we set off to find enough berries to make a strawberry torte. Of course, it all depending on borrowing an egg, then getting a little flour from the mill owner, then . . . but first, the strawberries! No larger than my fingernail, these delicate morsels grew low on the ground and were hard to pick. And they hid under leaves. It would not be too long before I tired of the search. Hannelore would sit me on a tree stump, fill my hands with berries, and let me munch while she carried on hunting alone. She is still a good sister and still my favorite!

All summer long, the forest and fields would share their treasures with us. Walking along the creek, we picked peppermint. Camilla grew in certain meadows – we'd gather it wherever we found it, since it made an instant cure for winter tummy aches or sleeplessness. We'd tie little bundles with string into bouquets and hang them in the attic to dry. We'd find a plant called Common Horsetail, too, which has amazing cleansing powers

and can clean almost anything, even copper. In those days, we had to learn how to make the best use of everything we could find, for in post-war Germany the stores were empty of things to buy.

My goodness, I almost forgot about Oscar, my spotted bunny. Mama came home with a skinny little rabbit, ready to be fattened into a nice Sunday roast. She soon had to give up on that idea, once I made that bunny my own. I would pick clover and dandelions for him, and he would let me brush his coat with a hairbrush. He was fun to chase around the garden, but cuddling on his soft fur was the part I liked best!

If there was nothing ripe for picking, then it was time to go swimming. My sister would sometimes take me to the town of Donaueschingen, about two hours bicycle ride away, where a little stream emerges from the ground. It soon joins two rivers to form the Danube, but our swim area was very shallow. For me, the best part of going swimming – ha, I never did learn to swim – was hopping from rock to rock, catching frogs.

Cherry-time! I'd pick the prettiest, roundest double-stemmed cherries and

Make the Picture Window

1   Follow the directions on pages 2 to 3 to transfer the entire image inside the picture window onto fabric. Trace the pattern onto tracing paper first, then use graphite paper to transfer the design to fabric. Work carefully, tracing one section at a time.

Background

2   Begin with the curving line between the sky and the mountains. Transfer this line onto both blue and grey fabric. Check against the master template to make sure that both fabric lines match *exactly*. Trim each piece to a ⅛" seam allowance. (See page 4 for help with cutting and seam allowances.) Turn under the seam allowance as you go, and appliqué the upper edge of the grey mountain piece on top of the blue sky piece. You will need to clip curves as you sew, so that the appliqué lies neatly on top of the blue fabric. (See page 4 for help with appliqué.)

3   In the same way, trace, transfer, then appliqué the bottom edge of the mountains on top of the light green fabric that forms the grass. Next, appliqué the bottom edge of the grass on top of the blue pond fabric. Complete the background by tracing, transferring, and appliquéing the dull green pond-side fabric on top of the bottom edge of the blue pond fabric.

4   Check the size of the background against the master template. It should measure about 21¼" wide x 26" from the bottom to the center top. Allow an extra ½" seam allowance all around, then trim away any excess fabric. If necessary, turn the work over and trim away any excess fabric to a scant ⅛ " seam allowance. This will help reduce any bulky layers your needle has to work through later when you quilt.

Sieglinde's Secret

I prefer to completely finish tracing and transferring the image to fabric before I begin any sewing. If you are less patient and can't wait to pick up your needle, complete the entire background, then choose distinct areas of the quilt to concentrate on first. Take care to note, however, which pieces should be appliquéd before others (see page 4).

Appliqués

5   As you become more familiar with my techniques, you will be able to choose any part of the design to begin your appliqué. Until you have completed one quilt, I suggest you begin by building the picture from the bottom up. Start by studying the bottom 7" or so of the picture window, across the entire width (up to the peak of the green boy's hat). If you have not completed tracing and transferring the motifs in this area to fabric, do so now. Working from left to right, cut pieces (adding a ⅛" seam allowance or smaller for the tiny pieces) for the pink flower, the sitting boy, the lily pads and stems, the pink girl with lily, the orange girl with flower, the waterbug, and the dull green patch at the far right. Cut the entire length of each long reed. (Note that the children's faces, hair, hands, and feet, plus the waterbug's legs and antennae are embroidered; you will not have to cut appliqués for these pieces.) Study the photograph to figure out the appliqué sequence (see also page 4). Here, for instance, the three lily pads and the patch of dull green at the far right go down first, followed by the children and the bugs. Appliqué only the bottom 7" or so of the reeds, leaving the rest unfinished for now (since they will overlap pieces you have not yet sewn down). Turn the work over and trim away any excess fabric to reduce bulk.

6   Move to the next 6" section across the width of the pattern (just above the head of the yellow girl). Working from left to right, cut pieces (adding ⅛" seam allowance) for the purple girl, the blue girl, the dull green/brown boy, the waterbug, the bright green girl and the yellow girl. Starting with the children, appliqué each piece onto the background (be sure to sew the boy's pants and sweater before adding his cloak). Sew the next 6" or so of the long reeds, taking care to overlap them onto other motifs, as in the photograph. Note that you will not be able to finish appliquéing the reed that overlaps the yellow girl's hair until the embroidery is complete. Turn the work over and trim away any excess fabric to reduce bulk.

7   Move to the next 5½" section across the width of the pattern (up the point where the picture window angles inwards). Working from left to right, cut pieces (adding ⅛" seam allowance) for the blue and purple flowers, the stems and leaves, and the dragonfly. (Look carefully at the photograph to see that the

hang them over my ears, then march inside to show off my new earrings! When Mama was ready, I'd help her take the stones out of the delicious little cherry hearts – and I would usually eat more than was good for me!

In Summer, I got to be a farmer's helper, too. There I'd stand atop a horse-drawn wagon, stomping down the hay with my little feet. My reward? A hunk of bread topped with butter and homemade elderberry jam. I would always take my slice home, where it was cut into wedges and became cake for the whole family. I was so proud to be to such a big help and to see Mama smile.

Of course, Summer came with its share of chores, too. When the beans were ripe in the garden, I would have to pull strings from each and every one before Mama could can them for Winter. Try as I might, I could find

nothing fun to do with those boring old beans. When she saw I wasn't busy, Oma would try to get me to sit with her and sew or learn another handcraft. But in Summer there were just too many more exciting and, to my mind, more important things to do!

One duty I never overlooked, though, was writing to Papa, who spent most of the war years away from us. I "wrote" my first letter to Papa when I was three years old. Of course, my signature was just a child's scribble, and I sewed paper strips onto the top of the letter, hoping they looked like flowers. Mama translated my scribble at the bottom of my message, but even without that, I think Papa knew exactly what I wanted to say.

Sieglinde's Secret

When working on the little boy on the left, begin sewing the bottoms of the reeds behind him before sewing his cloak. Appliqué his pants before working on his cloak, too. Remember that the first-sewn pieces recede from the eye, while the last-sewn pieces appear to come forward (see page 4).

flower centers, many of the stems, the brown-gold grass at the center, and the body of the dragonfly are embroidered, not appliquéd.) Start by appliquéing the reeds, noting where they overlap each other and making sure the underneath pieces are sewn in place first. Move on to the flowers, then the dragonfly. As before, leave unfinished any reeds that overlap unsewn or unembroidered sections of the design. Turn the work over and trim away any excess fabric to reduce bulk.

8   Complete the remaining top section of the picture window in the same way. Appliqué the reeds first, then the yellow flower. (Note that the spider, spider's web, and flower buds are embroidered, not appliqué.) Some elements of the design overlap the picture-window border; you will not be able to finish appliquéing the dragonfly wing at the far right or the blue flower and leaf at the far left until the border is done. Turn the work over and trim away any excess fabric to reduce bulk.

Embroider the Picture Window

10   Complete the layered embroidery of the children's faces, hair, hands, legs, and feet. Complete all other layered embroidery, such as details on the flowers and bugs. (For help with layered embroidery, see page 5.)

11   With single-strand black embroidery thread and stem stitch, outline all elements of the design. Outline around each child, each bug, each flower, each reed, and each stem. Study the photographs to see exactly where to outline. (For help with stem stitch embroidery, see page 7).

12   Use stem stitch to add details like the silver grey ripples on the water and on the pond-side, the black and grey spider web, the black, grey, and orange spider, the gold, black, and orange fern leaves, the teal and black dragonfly, the white and orange flower centers, the orange, yellow, and lilac buds, and the green stems. Add a little extra detail to the budding fern at the far right by embroidering French knots over it, (see page 6).

Make the Borders

13 See page 7 for directions on how to complete the narrow picture window border.

14 See page 7 for directions on how to make the wide outer border and attach it to the picture window.

15 Follow the directions on pages 2 to 3 to transfer the letters and flowers inside the wide border onto fabric. Trace onto tracing paper first, then use graphite paper to transfer the marks to fabric. Work carefully, tracing one section at a time.

16 Cut pieces (adding ⅛" seam allowance) for the letters at the top of the quilt, then applique them carefully in place. Do the same for the green and brown leaves, the pink and yellow flowers, and the ladybugs. Note any overlaps, particularly where the leaf at the left overlaps the picture-window border.

17 In the same way, cut pieces then appliqué the flowers, leaves, and buds along the left border and the bottom left corner.

18 Use layered embroidery to complete the leaves and buds, the wasps' bodies, the caterpillar, and detailing on the butterfly. Outline each appliqué and embroidery with stem stitch (see pages 5 to 6). Use French knots to complete the orange buds on the top leftmost purple/yellow flowers, the top rightmost blue flowers, and the bottom purple and blue flowers. Use lazy daisy stitch (see page 6) to detail the lilac flowers at the bottom. Stem stitch your autograph at the bottom right.

19 Follow the directions on pages 8 to 9 to add backing, quilt the entire piece, scallop the outer border, and add binding.

Fall Idyll

"But Autumn comes,
The storm clouds burst,
And rush the tots home,
To good Mother Earth."

The wind shifts and Fall is in the air. The
first dusty smell of Autumn takes me right
back to my childhood days in Germany.
The fields I knew so well are harvested,
and purple Asters and Golden Rod are
in bloom in the meadows. In the woods,
chestnuts, acorns, and pinecones litter
the ground. How excited I would be as

Finished size: 30½" x 36½", including binding

Materials

All quantities are generous so that you can cut large shapes from a single piece of fabric, wherever possible. You will have plenty of leftover fabric to play with! I used variegated batiks for everything except Mother Earth's cap and apron, and the white dress at the center of the quilt. There, I used shiny white polyester, which works well because of its sheen and texture.

Background

Sky: ½ yard light blue

Distant meadows: ¼ light brown, scrap of medium brown

Grass at riverbank: ¼ light green

Cave top: ¼ green-brown

Cave interior: ¼ dark brown

Path: ¼ medium brown

Grass at foreground: Scraps in three shades of green

Appliqués

Grass: ¼ yard each or large scraps in three shades of green and two shades of brown

Trees and roots: Large scraps in at least four shades of brown

Mother Earth: ¼ yard or large scraps of brown and white

Dresses, boy clothes, and cloaks: ⅛ yard each or large scraps of red, blue, white, and muted shades of blue, green, brown, and yellow

Bugs: Scraps of blue and purple

Letters, leaves, branches, and mushrooms: Large scraps in three shades each of orange, brown, and gold

Berries: Scraps of purple

Plus

Narrow picture-window border : 2½ yards black single-fold bias piping

Wide border: 1 yard light brown

Embroidery: Single-ply embroidery thread in black and white, as well as shades of silver grey, gold, yellow, orange, brown, cream, pink, lilac, and teal.

Note See page 2 for help in choosing fabrics

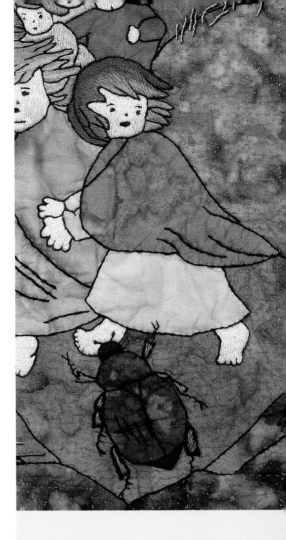

I gathered handfuls of them into the skirt of my dress. I would take them home and my sisters would help me make sweet little stick people from them.

Fall was a time for picking apples and nuts. What joy this brought to me when I was small! For me, there was nothing better than to pick an apple or pear right off the tree. I would cherish those sweet moments of anticipation before I would bite into it. Hazelnuts were another special treat. On the way to school I had to walk along a path was lined with Hazelnut bushes. I always wanted to be the first to pick those tasty morsels and share them with my special friends at lunchtime. It was good to be young; life was so simple then and so full of surprises!

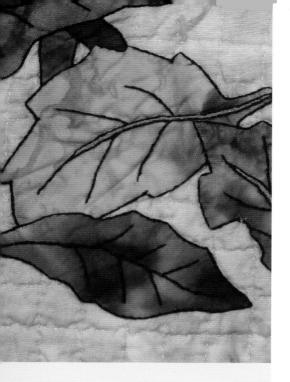

Fall was mushroom season, too. I would roam through the forest looking for those tasty treats. This chore was much more to my liking! I would find my favorite--wild Pfifferlinge, or chanterelles. Mama would use them to make a special German pasta dish called Spaetzle. It was a meal fit for princesses!

Fall was a time for chores, too. Papa was away most of the war and post-war years. He spent several years as a prisoner of war, and Mama was left to run our busy household alone. She always had her hands full, and we children had to help wherever we could. Since we were a family of four children and two adults, we were allowed to "glean" the fields in Fall. What is gleaning? After the crops were harvested, we would crawl through the farmer's muddy fields on hands and knees to find new potatoes to take home for our family. This was not much fun, but I always managed to find some sort of entertainment for myself. You see, sometimes if I was lucky, I would find a nest of pink, newly born field mice to play with. Of course, I tried

Make the Picture Window

1   Follow the directions on pages 2 to 3 to transfer the entire image inside the picture window onto fabric. Trace the pattern onto tracing paper first, then use graphite paper to transfer the design to fabric. Work carefully, tracing one section at a time.

Background

2   Begin with the curving line that separates the sky from the cave top at the left and the distant meadows at the left and across the center. Transfer this line onto blue (sky), green-brown (cave top) and light brown (distant meadows). Check against the master template to make sure that both fabric lines match *exactly*. Trim each piece to a ⅛" seam allowance. (See page 4 for help with cutting and seam allowances).Turn under the seam allowance as you go, and appliqué the upper edge of the light brown meadow piece on top of the blue sky piece. You will need to clip curves as you sew, so that the appliqué lies neatly on top of the blue fabric. (See page 4 for help with appliqué.) Next, appliqué the cave top piece on top of the sky piece, noting that it overlaps slightly onto the meadows.

3   In the same way, trace, transfer, then appliqué the bottom edge of the cave top of the dark brown fabric that forms the cave interior. Appliqué a small piece of medium-brown fabric on top of the distant meadows. Follow this with pieces of green for the grass, then blue for the river, then brown for the strip immediately below the river. Begin the foreground by tracing, transferring, and appliquéing the green-brown fabric that forms the children's wide path and the green fabric at the far right. To complete the background, trace, transfer, and appliqué shapes in three shades of green to form the bottom edge of the picture window.

4   Check the size of the background against the master template. It should measure about 22" wide x 26" from the bottom to the center top. Allow an extra ½" seam allowance all around, then trim away any excess fabric. If necessary, turn the work over and trim away any excess fabric to a scant ⅛" seam allowance. This will help reduce any bulky layers your needle has to work through later when you quilt.

Sieglinde's Secret

Look carefully at the background to see how many shades of green, green-brown, light-brown, and medium brown form the meadows, the grass, and the children's path. The more shades of each color you use, the richer your background will be.

Appliqués

5   As you become more familiar with my techniques, you will be able to choose any part of the design to begin your appliqué. Until you have completed one quilt, I suggest you begin by building the picture from the bottom up. Start by studying the bottom 7" or so of the picture window, across the entire width (to the top of Mother Earth's apron). If you have not completed tracing and transferring the motifs in this area to fabric, do so now. Cut pieces for the roots and the tree trunk at the far right (adding a ⅛" seam allowance or smaller). Appliqué the first 7" or so of the tree trunk in place, leaving the rest unfinished for now. Appliqué the leftmost section of roots in place. Begin appliquéing the large root that stretches across the center of the picture window. Leave the topmost branch of the root unfinished for now, since it overlaps onto the blue dress, the yellow dress, and the blue bug. Working from left to right, cut pieces (adding seam allowance) for Mother Earth's dress and apron, the blue girl, and the purple bug. (Note that the children's faces, hair, hands and feet, plus the bug's legs and antennae are embroidered; you will not have to cut appliqués for these pieces.) Study the photograph to figure out the appliqué sequence (see also page 4). Here, for instance, Mother Earth's dress goes down first, followed by her apron, then the blue dress. Leave the bug's head unfinished, since it overlaps onto a child's embroidered foot. Turn the work over and trim away any excess fabric to reduce bulk.

6   Move to the next 6" section across the width of the pattern (just above Mother Earth's head). Start with the small tree trunk at the right, then finish sewing the next four inches or so of the large tree trunk, stopping where it overlaps onto an embroidered leaf at the right. Next, move on to the tiny green hoods of the most distant children, immediately to the left of the small tree trunk. Work forwards, completing all the green hoods and the red girl. Note that my yellow and light blue girls at the back of the line are embroidered. If you prefer to appliqué them, cut pieces and do so. Appliqué the dark blue dress, then the green/pink cloak, then the yellow dress and brown cloak. Next appliqué the boy in brown and green, plus his flower stem. Move further left to appliqué the light blue girl next, followed by the mustard yellow girl, the white girl, then the foremost boy in the green cloak. Appliqué the rest of Mother Earth's brown dress in place, then appliqué the green and red girl. Appliqué Mother Earth's cap, the blue bug, and the ladybug. Turn the work over and trim away any excess fabric to reduce bulk.

to take them home instead of the potatoes, but my sister always kept an eye on me.

One of my favorite pastimes was to collect pretty fallen leafs. I would take them home and carefully press them between newspapers. Then I would set bricks on top of this newspaper sandwich and wait a few days until the leaves were dry and perfectly flat. With mounting excitement, I would take a stiff brush and gently hit the leaf. In an instant, the magic happened! All the leaf material would fall away, leaving the delicate veins of the leaf behind.

Though you might not know it, we celebrate our own version of Thanksgiving Day in Germany, too. Farmers would choose some of the very best fruits of their harvest and

Sieglinde's Secret

To achieve the effect of the line of children rushing from a distance up to the cave, work from the back of the queue to the front. This will make the children at the back recede from the eye, while those at the front appear to come forward (see page 4). Look carefully at the photographs to see exactly where the overlaps are, then determine your sewing sequence.

7   Move to the next 6" section across the width of the pattern (just below the tree trunk on the cave top). Working from left to right, cut pieces (adding ⅛" seam allowance or smaller) for the roots inside the cave and any branches you have not yet cur for the small tree at the right. Note that my falling leaves as well as the small trees at the center of the picture are embroidered; if you prefer to appliqué them, cut pieces now. Appliqué all these pieces in place, noting any overlaps and sewing down the back pieces first. Turn the work over and trim away any excess fabric to reduce bulk.

8   Complete the remaining top section of the picture window in the same way. Complete the large tree at the right, leaving unfinished any sections where embroidered leaves fall behind the branches. Cut then appliqué pieces for the light brown tree at the left. Turn the work over and trim away any excess fabric to reduce bulk.

Embroider the Picture Window

10 Complete the layered embroidery of the children's faces, hair, hands, legs and feet. Embroider Mother Earth's face and hands, plus her silver keys and gold key chain. Complete all other layered embroidery, including all of the leaves and the ladybug's spots. (For help with layered embroidery, see page 5.)

11 With single-strand black embroidery thread and stem stitch, outline all elements of the design. Outline around each child, each bug, each leaf, each root, and each branch. Study the photographs to see exactly where to outline. (For help with stem stitch embroidery, see page 7.)

12 Use stem stitch to add details like the tufts of grass, the thin roots, and the distant tree branches. Notice that the grass on the cave top uses a double line of black and yellow thread. Use lazy daisy stitch for the dandelion seeds at the center of the picture. Add French knots to embellish the bug's antennae. (See also page 6.)

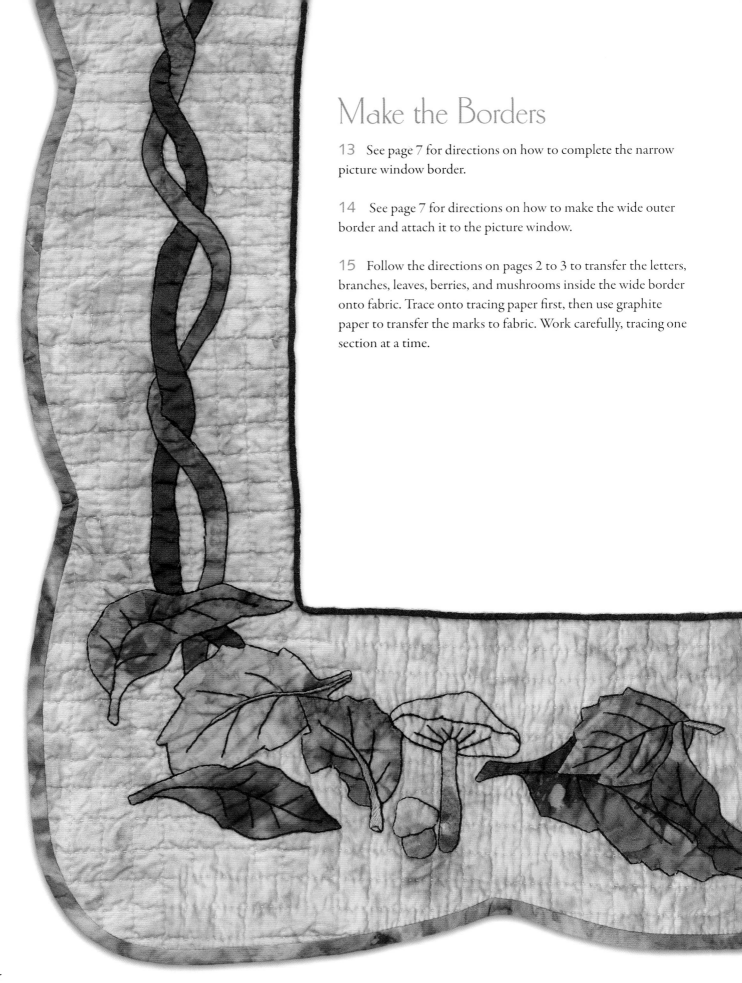

Make the Borders

13   See page 7 for directions on how to complete the narrow picture window border.

14   See page 7 for directions on how to make the wide outer border and attach it to the picture window.

15   Follow the directions on pages 2 to 3 to transfer the letters, branches, leaves, berries, and mushrooms inside the wide border onto fabric. Trace onto tracing paper first, then use graphite paper to transfer the marks to fabric. Work carefully, tracing one section at a time.

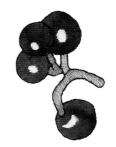

16 Cut pieces (adding ⅛" seam allowance) for the letters at the top of the quilt, then appliqué them carefully in place. Do the same for the branches, leaves, berries, and mushrooms. Note any overlaps, particularly the braiding of the branches, plus the leaf at the left that overlaps the picture-window border.

17 Use stem stitch to outline the letters, branches, leaves, berries, and mushrooms. Stem stitch your autograph at the bottom right.

18 Follow the directions on pages 8 to 9 to add backing and quilt the entire piece. Note the curved lines of stitching on Mother Earth's cap. Scallop the outer border, and add binding.

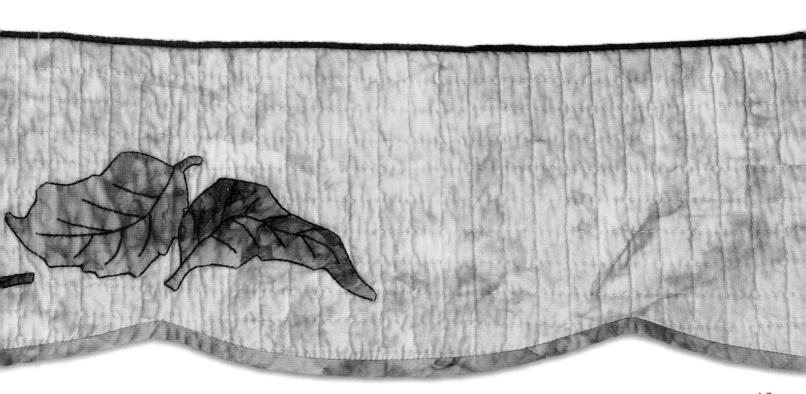

"Now off to bed
My little ones,
Sweet dreams until
The next year comes!"

It's November and the first snowflakes
are falling! With a satchel full of apples,
I headed off to school. Tradition had it
that on the first day it snowed, we were
allowed to bring apples to school and lay
them on top of the radiators. By lunchtime

Finished size: 30" x 37½", including binding

Winter

Sieglinde 2007

Materials

All quantities are generous so that you can cut large shapes from a single piece of fabric, wherever possible. You will have plenty of leftover fabric to play with! Since the colors of winter are quite subdued, I used muted shades of cotton batiks for everything except Mother Earth's cap, apron, and socks, the beams around the candles, and the tops of the tree stumps. For those, I used shiny white polyester. Note that the roofs of the distant houses are a muted white cotton.

Background

Sky: ½ yard light blue
Mountains: Scraps of grey-blue
Snow fields: ¼ yard or large scrap of cream
Cave: ½ yard dark brown

Appliqués

Trees, roots, and stumps: Large scraps in at least four shades of brown

Distant houses: Small scraps in cream and white

Children's clothes and Mother Earth's dress and shoes: Various shades of brown and reddish brown

Mother Earth's cap, apron, and socks, candle beams, tops of stumps: Scraps of white

Sewing basket: Scraps of brown, orange, pink, and blue

Bugs: Scraps of blue

Dresses and boy clothes: ⅛ yard each or large scraps of yellow, bright green, dull green, light blue, purple, orange, and pink

Poinsettias: Scraps of bright red, pink, and at least three shades of green

Letters: Scraps of at least three shades of blue

Plus

Narrow picture-window border: 2½ yards dark brown single-fold bias piping

Wide border: 1 yard cream

Embroidery: Single-ply embroidery thread in black and white, as well as shades of silver, gold, red, green, yellow, brown blue and grey

Note See page 2 for help in choosing fabrics.

–fried apples! Stomping through the woods on my way back home, I would follow tracks in the snow in hopes of discovering where the woodland creatures lived. Along the way, I could find so many interesting things to see and even more to imagine. Red and blue berries, capped with snow, would peep out of leafless bushes. Ha, what fun! In my mind's eye, I would see little faces on those berries, their bonnets dancing in the wind. The pine trees, with their arms outstretched, wore their winter attire, too. As if by magic, each new snowfall transformed them. The heavy loads of snow sculpted new figures—see, here is the wicked old witch who captured Hansel and Gretel. Right beside her stand the seven dwarfs! I still wonder if Hans Christian Andersen saw the trees that way, and if their weird and wonderful shapes ever inspired the characters in his stories.

Soon it would be Christmas. An Advent calendar reminded us how little time was left until the big day. Now

Oma took charge of my life. In those days we did not buy gifts; everything had to be made by hand. Every day after school we would sit together singing Christmas carols and work with Oma on our surprises. A pair of gloves for one sister, a scarf for another; they were simple gifts, but made with much effort and love! In the Germany of my childhood, there was no Santa Claus, but Saint Nikolaus made an appearance every December 6. He was not quite as jolly as today's Santa; always he is portrayed as the bishop that he was in real life. He carries a bishop's staff and a large golden book, in which he records the names of all the good children. He rewards their good deeds with "Gutzle", such as apples, nuts, and other small goodies. At his side is "Knecht Ruprecht", who carries a black book in which evil deeds are recorded. For those that had yet to learn to behave, it was fingernail-biting time. How did Saint Nikolaus know so much about so many children? Was Knecht Ruprecht going to take out the switch from his bag?

The Christkind, or Christ child, Himself does all the giving on

Make the Picture Window

1   Follow the directions on pages 2 to 3 to transfer the entire image inside the picture window onto fabric. Trace the pattern onto tracing paper first, then use graphite paper to transfer the design to fabric. Work carefully, tracing one section at a time.

Background

2   Begin with the curving line that separates the sky from the grey-blue mountains. Transfer this line onto light blue (sky) and grey-blue (mountains). Check against the master template to make sure that both fabric lines match *exactly*. Trim each piece to a ⅛" seam allowance. (See page 4 for help with cutting and seam allowances).Turn under the seam allowance as you go, and appliqué the upper edge of the grey-blue mountain piece on top of the light blue sky piece. You will need to clip curves as you sew, so that the appliqué lies neatly on top of the blue fabric. (See page 4 for help with appliqué.) Next, appliqué the cream meadow piece on top of the mountain piece, then the dark brown cave piece on top of the meadows. Note that the topmost line of tree roots will later hide this seam.

3   Check the size of the background against the master template. It should measure about 21" wide x 26" from the bottom to the center top. Allow an extra ½" seam allowance all around, then trim away any excess fabric. If necessary, turn the work over and trim away any excess fabric to a scant ⅛" seam allowance. This will help reduce any bulky layers your needle has to work through later when you quilt.

Sieglinde's Secret

If you wish, make the mountains out of scraps rather than a single piece of fabric. Trace, transfer, then cut these smaller appliqués one at a time. Look carefully at the photographs to decide which pieces to lay down first. Remember, the first-sewn pieces will recede into the background, while the last-sewn pieces will appear to advance toward the eye.

Christmas Eve. What excitement there would be in our house! Oh, how I longed to see that precious Child, but no matter how hard I tried, I never managed it! Though times were meager, this fact had absolutely no impact on our merriment, especially not mine! Would you believe that I was eight years old before I ever tasted chocolate, oranges, or bananas? Still, Mama always managed to create one of her little miracles and make something sweet, be it a cake made with cream of wheat instead of flour and sweetened with syrup made from sugar-beets. It most likely tasted different, but if it did, I was not aware of it. To me everything was magic about Christmas and I might add it still is to date. And yes, to my husband Bill's dismay, I still have burning candles on my tree. Poor Bill, he always stands by with a fire-extinguisher, but please don't tell the fire-marshal – our house insurance might go up!

Christmas was also time to set up the Puppet-theater and the dollhouse. We were not allowed to play with these items out of doors. The main character of the puppets was a fellow called "Kasperle". Supporting roles were "Grossmutti" (grandma), brother Seppel, and a Crocodile. Every year

Appliqués

4   As you become more familiar with my techniques, you will be able to choose any part of the design to begin your appliqué. Until you have completed one quilt, I suggest you begin by building the picture from the bottom up. Start by studying the bottom 5" or so of the picture window, across the entire width (to the top of the threesome of sleeping children at the far left). If you have not completed tracing and transferring the motifs in this area to fabric, do so now. Cut pieces for the lower roots, Mother Earth's dress, apron, shoes and socks, and the three bugs (adding a ⅛" seam allowance or smaller). Working from left to right, appliqué the tree roots in place. Appliqué the three children's clothes, starting with the boy at the back, the girl at the left, then the boy at the right. Appliqué Mother Earth's sock then shoe, followed by her dress and apron. Appliqué the three bugs and their candle beams in place.

5   Move to the next 7" section across the width of the pattern (just above the head of the topmost child). Start with the roots, appliquéing each in place across the width of the quilt. Look carefully at the photographs to see the sequence in which the children's brown outfits are sewn down. Begin with the yawning boy at the left, then the child immediately below him and the two sleeping children on the topmost branch. Next, appliqué the rightmost child, then work forwards to complete the three remaining children in turn. Continue sewing down Mother Earth's dress and apron. Notice that the sewing basket loops behind her arm, so be sure to appliqué the small back section of the basket handle before finishing her sleeve. Appliqué the rest of the sewing basket, completing the fabrics before the large basket piece and the rest of the handle. Appliqué the ladybugs. Turn the work over and trim away any excess fabric to reduce bulk.

6   Move to the next 6" section across the width of the pattern (to the top of the cave). Cut pieces for and appliqué all the roots, including the light brown roots that stretch across the width of the quilt. Complete Mother Earth's dress and cap, noting where they overlap the roots. Turn the work over and trim away any excess fabric to reduce bulk.

7   Complete the remaining top section of the picture window in the same way. Cut pieces for the large trees and appliqué in place, avoiding areas where embroideries are tucked behind the appliqués. Do not sew down any of the branches or sections of trunk that overlap into the wide border. Appliqué the snow-topped tree stumps. Cut pieces for the houses and appliqué them in place. Note that all my animals are embroidered; if you prefer to use appliqué, cut pieces and appliqué those down, too. Turn the work over and trim away any excess fabric to reduce bulk.

we would write another epic of Kasperle's life and tribulations and perform it for our parents. I still have three of these puppets.

In our home, before we were allowed to open our presents, we first had to bring our gifts to the Baby in the manger. After all, it is His Birthday not ours. What kind of gifts? We had to tell the story of His birth, say prayers, recite poems, sing songs, and play the piano for the Baby Jesus. For this purpose, Mama would dress us girls as angels. Dressed in long white dresses, gathered with golden belts, and wearing golden halos and wings, we felt ever so special— almost holy—well, as holy as any child can possibly be!

After what seemed to be forever, we were allowed to present our gifts to our parents, after which, it was finally our turn. At last, we were allowed to see what this most Holy Bearer of gifts had brought to all of us children.

Embroider the Picture Window

8   Complete the layered embroidery of the children's faces, hair, hands, legs and feet. Embroider Mother Earth's face and hands, plus her silver keys and gold key chain. Complete all other layered embroidery, including the bugs' legs, the ladybugs' spots, the candles and candle trays, the scissors, the deer, the bunny, the squirrel, the bird, the distant trees, and the house details. (For help with layered embroidery, see page 5.)

9   With single-strand black embroidery thread and stem stitch, outline all elements of the design. Outline around each child, each bug, each root, each branch, and each woodland creature. Study the photographs to see exactly where to outline. (For help with stem stitch embroidery, see page 7.)

10   Use stem stitch to add details like the thin roots, the distant tree branches, the basket weave, the bugs' antennae, the fences, details on the woodland creatures, and the candlelight. Notice that the grass on the cave top uses a double line of black and yellow thread. Use lazy daisy stitch for the dandelion seeds at the center of the picture. Add French knots to embellish the bugs' antennae and details on the woodland creatures. (See also page 6.)

Make the Borders

11 See page 7 for directions on how to complete the narrow picture window border.

12 See page 7 for directions on how to make the wide outer border and attach it to the picture window.

13 Follow the directions on pages 2 to 3 to transfer the letters, branches, and poinsettias inside the wide border onto fabric. Trace onto tracing paper first, then use graphite paper to transfer the marks to fabric. Work carefully, tracing one section at a time.

14 Cut pieces (adding ⅛" seam allowance) for the letters at the top of the quilt, then appliqué them carefully in place. Do the same for the branches. Note any overlaps, particularly where the branches weave in and out of the letters and where they overlap the picture-window border.

15 Use stem stitch to outline the letters, flowers, and branches in black. Add an extra row of white stem stitch to outline the branches, giving an impression of snow. Use layered embroidery to complete the poinsettia berries, flower centers, and stems, as well as the owl. Outline each appliqué and embroidery with stem stitch (see page 6). Use French knots to make black dots at the center of each berry and for the owl's black pupils. Stem stitch your autograph at the bottom right.

16 Follow the directions on pages 8 to 9 to add backing and quilt the entire piece. Note the straight lines of stitching on Mother Earth's cap and apron. Scallop the outer border, and add binding.

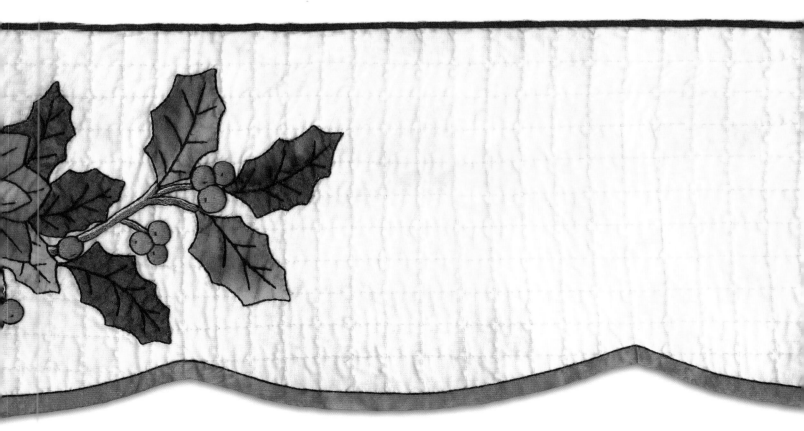

Also by Sieglinde Schoen Smith

Mother Earth and Her Children: A Quilted Fairy Tale
A charming picture book for young children, celebrating the miracles of nature in the changing seasons. Winner of the American Horticultural Society's *Growing Good Kids Book Award.*
ISBN: 978-1933308-18-0, 32 pages, hardcover with jacket

Mother Earth's ABC: A Quilter's Alphabet and Storybook
A delightful romp from A to Z, telling the story of a seed's miraculous Spring awakening. Beautiful appliqué letters are ready to trace and sew into quilting projects.
ISBN: 978-1-933308-20-3, 40 pages, hardcover with jacket

Mother Earth's ABCs: Photo-Transfer Pack and CD
An easy way to reproduce Sieglinde's illustrated alphabet: resize, arrange, and print onto fabric sheets. Requires design/picture editing software.
UPC: 8-82383-00029-3, CD plus 5 fabric sheets

Mother Earth and Her Children: Jigsaw Puzzle and Poster
Recreate the images in Sieglinde's award-winning quilt, one puzzle piece at a time. Includes a folded poster of *Mother Earth and Her Children.*
ISBN: 978-1-933308-24-1, 750 piece jigsaw puzzle plus poster (27" x 16½")

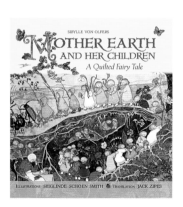

For more information contact Breckling Press at 630-941-1179   (800-951-7836)
or visit www.brecklingpress.com